Life Is like a
Book of Sudoku

	4	6						
9		2		6				8
	8		4			2	5	
			8				7	
5			7		2			3
	1				6			
	6	4				3	9	
3				8		1		2
						7	3	

Life Is like a Book of Sudoku

4	6							
9	2		6					8
	8	4			2	5		
		8				7		
5			7		2			3
	1				6			
	6	4			3	9		
3				8		1		2
						7	3	

A Practical Guide to
Achieve a Balanced Life

Harold J Angus

PARTRIDGE
A Penguin Random House Company

To order additional copies of this book, contact
Toll Free 800 101 2657 (Singapore)
Toll Free 1 800 81 7340 (Malaysia)
orders.singapore@partridgepublishing.com

www.partridgepublishing.com/singapore

Contents

For My Beloved Patricia

Foreword

I am delighted to write the Foreword for Life Is Like A Book Of Sudoku by my friend Harold Angus.

Here is an approach to good common sense in understanding and living this life we have been gifted with.

Harold delves into observations and personal experience he has gathered and noted through the years.

While books of such genre tend to be preachy and filled with lofty idealism, he manages to encourage and urge the reader to a richer life in a disarming manner.

He talks straight and does not apologize for his frank advice.

However, he backs each piece of advice with proven badge-earned snippets of lessons in life. The reader feels together with him with each new revelation from his own heart.

This warm approach is reminiscent of the writings of a favourite author of mine, Keith Miller, of "Habitation of Dragons" fame.

The use of a "Matrix", a rather helpful utilization of mnemonics, to introduce each sub-topic he empathically deals with, reminds us of the classic Johari Window of Understanding. Yet, Harold leads the Reader to a different paradigm; and we gladly follow him down this path of knowledge.

An everyday man speaks to his fellow everyday friends, and invites all to the joy of seeing Life as a Book of Sudoku.

I would recommend it to every family, for the issues sensitively discussed within are practical and wise for daily application in the family context.

David TC Loo
Retired Pastor, Methodist Church in Malaysia
Founder President, Emmanuel Golden Years Communities
(A Retirement Community Ministry)
Council Member, Malaysian Healthy Ageing Society
Kuala Lumpur, Malaysia
4th July 2014

Introduction

Life is getting complicated these days with so many new inventions that impact our lives.

If an alien were to visit Earth and report back to his mother ship, he would probably say:

"Earthlings are strange creatures, they always carry a small object that is plugged into their ears and some have even fallen into holes as they do not look where they are going!

They even use this gadget when they drive mechanised boxes at great speed and many people have been killed in collisions.

Furthermore some also inject themselves with unknown substances that make them move in a frenzied state to extremely loud music, just like robots until they collapse.

It appears that they may not be as intelligent as we thought!

I do not recommend that we invade this planet as the inhabitants show an inferior intelligence and we may compromise our safety".

Maybe our behaviour as observed by aliens will save us from an invasion?

Life is becoming even more complex with technological and economic advances that we may lose sight of some values that are important to lead a balanced life and enable us to fulfill our dreams.

This book will help you to understand the many facets of our life and that is why the title is "Life is Like a Book of Sudoku".

List of Illustrations

Notes:

All illustrations and cover designed by Harold J Angus
All illustrations except #8 drawn by alaistarlaird from fiverr.com
#8 drawn by frank82 from fiverr.com

Life is Like a Sudoku Puzzle

S<small>TOP</small>!

If you have not done a Sudoku puzzle before, please try and solve a simple Sudoku puzzle before you read any further or you will not fully appreciate the message in this book.

Rules for Sudoku:

A Sudoku puzzle will take maybe 10 minutes or more if you are good with numbers but the more complex ones could take hours or even days. The rules to solving are simple: there are nine small squares arranged inside a larger square and each small square is divided into nine smaller squares. What you need to do is to fill up the numbers from 1 to 9 inside the squares so that no number is repeated inside the small squares and also horizontally and vertically in the large square. Some numbers are given in each Sudoku puzzle so that you can solve the puzzle.

(Diagonal squares are not considered in Sudoku)

	4	6						
9		2		6				8
		8	4			2	5	
			8				7	
5			7		2			3
	1				6			
	6	4			3	9		
3				8		1		2
						7	3	

Illustration 2. SUDOKU Puzzle

(Rating: very easy; target 6 minutes)

I have been doing Sudoku puzzles for a few years now and have developed my own techniques for solving the more difficult puzzles. However, this book is not about these techniques but how solving a Sudoku puzzle is akin to understanding and tackling the problems in everyday life.

Hence the title is derived from the movie Forest Gump where he said: "Life is like a Box of Chocolates".

I believe that "Life is like a Book of Sudoku" is a more accurate saying to depict life.

The following qualities are necessary to solve a puzzle:

1. You need to be focussed.
2. You need to be persistent.
3. You realise that all the numbers are important and need to be put in their proper places.
4. You need to change your decisions when you make mistakes.
5. It is best that you solve your puzzle yourself and not rely too heavily on others.
6. Sometimes, taking a short break will help you to solve the puzzle faster.
7. If you give up on the puzzle, you will NEVER solve it.
8. When you are sure of any number, you need to fill it in the proper space so that the puzzle can be completed.
9. For the more difficult puzzles, you can reach a stage where you need to try out certain numbers to progress. These numbers should be tested using pencil or the puzzle becomes very messy!
10. Once you mess up the puzzle with a permanent marker, it becomes more difficult to solve.

Aren't all these also related to living a life of happiness and fulfilment?

If this is your first Sudoku puzzle, the manner in which you approach the solution can reflect how you tackle life's problems.

Some folks ignore it as it is something new and they don't want to try it. They wait to see how others fare. These are the people who dare not evaluate new opportunities and take some risks.

Some attack the puzzle with great gusto and end up in a mess as many mistakes are made. They take action without much thinking.

A few are the opposite and take a lot of time to examine the puzzle from every angle before they take any action.

Some will start the puzzle, lose interest and do other things instead. They avoid doing the puzzle for as long as possible.

So in which category do you fall under?

No one leads a life that is perfect and change is constant.

You can consider life to be a series of Sudoku puzzles, each is unique and there is only one solution to each puzzle.

Just as you cannot solve some Sudoku puzzles, in life it is impossible to maintain a state of perfect happiness. We are always striving for more. An unsolved Sudoku puzzle is like that - you might get 80% of the answers right and may not be able to get the remaining numbers.

Even after you manage to solve one puzzle, you need to move on to another puzzle which will have a different set of clues. Similarly, life is always changing and we constantly need to adapt.

Now let us examine how the life matrix can be applied to a Sudoku puzzle.

You will notice that a Sudoku puzzle has nine squares with one central square. I call this the CORE.

Family	Spirituality	Career
Finances	**CORE**	Society
Health	Education	Recreation

Illustration 3. How your CORE influences the Other Areas

So what did you notice about the Sudoku puzzle that you solved?

Notes

What exactly is the CORE?

You are unique and there is no one exactly like you among the 7 billion inhabitants on this planet. Your CORE is your unique identity, made up of the qualities you have developed in your life, tempered by your disposition at the different phases of your life and influenced by the many factors that pull or push you to make decisions on a continuous basis.

The CORE is the essence of your being. It is what represents you and no one else. It is the embodiment of the values you hold dear and your personality traits. Your CORE will usually influence the other eight areas in your life.

Those numbers given in each puzzle can be considered some things in life that you cannot change, like your parents, your DNA, the town where you were born and your health conditions. Without those few numbers, one cannot solve the puzzle.

How you treat the given numbers is how you are influenced by the CORE of your life at that point in time.

Even your siblings will have a different CORE from you, though they share many of your factors. For one, they react differently to the same situation for we all have a different approach to life. And that is what makes life interesting.

The eight areas around your CORE are:

1. Family
2. Spirituality
3. Career
4. Finances
5. Society
6. Health
7. Education
8. Recreation

The importance of each area is not fixed; different areas will take precedence at different stages of your life.

For example, education is very important in the school-going ages up into university after which you will start to develop a career.

Then when you retire and grow old, health and financial issues may dominate your life.

Your CORE may also adjust as your values and beliefs may be changed based on your life experiences, social pressures and norms. For example, in early adulthood, the social area becomes important when you go out to meet friends as you are considering marriage and raising a family.

If you look at the overall Sudoku puzzle, you will realise that life is a Matrix of different areas and each area needs proper order and balance so that your life is not in a state of chaos.

Each area in your life is not isolated and some areas overlap such as a good career will impact your financial position and your education level will determine the type of job you will be qualified to do.

Life is really a matrix of decisions, actions and results in the different areas and your life will be balanced for a while if you make the correct decisions that produce the desired results. But even achieving success means that your life changes again. The only way to be happy in life is to expect and embrace change!

When you did your Sudoku puzzle, how did you find the process of solving it? Was it enjoyable or dreadful?

Maybe it was a mixture of emotions?

For some numbers and squares, it is a joy to fill in the spaces correctly and yet when you are stuck for a long time, you get frustrated.

Did you notice that the problem is easier to solve when you used the easier numbers to fill up the squares? Some squares are easier to solve but to solve the Sudoku matrix you depend on inputs from other squares. You need to fill as many numbers as possible so you can figure out the rest.

Life is like that too. When things go well, life is a pleasure but when problems arise, the pleasure turns to pain.

Procrastination is a habit with many people and the author confesses to such a weakness. Some problems in life are easy to solve and yet we take ages to act. Just like not filling the numbers you know in the Sudoku puzzle, procrastination in life saps your energy and makes the bigger problems even more difficult to solve. Have you ever experienced this phenomenon?

Your life is miserable and there are so many issues to settle. Then you decide to take some decisive actions for the outstanding issues. Suddenly the field clears and you are able to easily tackle all the outstanding problems.

This would be like the "try out" numbers in the Sudoku puzzle. Sometimes a puzzle is difficult to solve unless you try a given solution. In life, it could be a decision like wanting to start a business. You may want to keep your job until the business is properly established.

In life, you cannot simply ignore your problems as most require action on your part. No one can live your life as each person's life is unique and entirely different from everyone else's. So you need to confront the problems and take positive steps to overcome them.

For example: if your results are not good in school, you need to find out if you have put in enough effort into your studies, especially the weaker subjects. No point moaning over bad marks if you have not been paying attention in class and not doing the assignments.

All the eight areas surrounding the CORE are well known and you can research them in greater detail elsewhere.

I do not proclaim to be an expert in any of the eight areas but I would like to share my ideas and some of my own life experience on why and how they could affect your life.

In life, all the areas interact as life is a continuum of changing desires and priorities and often you have to multi-task to find the right balance.

(You can read the following chapters in any order that you wish)

Family Matters

"The most important thing a father can do for his children is to love their mother." **Theodore Hesburgh**

Each one of us is born in different circumstances. Some have adopted parents and some are born out of wedlock and may have been given away after birth. Be glad that you have the potential to achieve a life of fulfillment and purpose.

As a child, you have little choice but to obey your parents until you reach adolescence, after which you start to attain greater freedom. That is the ultimate challenge for every teenager.

Parents need to understand that arguments with teenage children are an inevitable sign of their maturing even though at the time we feel they are being "childish". Letting go is one of the difficult things that parents must learn. Many parents actually never "let go" of their children even though they have long left the roost.

Older children do argue with parents about boy-girl relationships, curfew, studies and a host of life-related problems.

Illustration 4. Try to spend time with your loved ones before it is too late.

My own experience:

I will relate one painful episode in which I confronted my father when we were having so many money problems and I was in secondary school at Form 5 and worried about my future. My father told me that he did not have an answer to his money problems. In anger I told him I just wondered why he had bothered to have so many children.

He just kept quiet and I knew that had hurt him deeply. He could have replied: "I should have stopped at two" but he just kept a grave silence. I was his third son. After that episode, I never asked him about money anymore.

My mother was not highly educated but she cooked and cleaned for five sons. She did not understand the subjects we learned in school but she always encouraged us to "study hard".

We were living opposite a church in Ipoh and she worked part-time in a nearby hospital laundry for a few years but the work was too heavy and she developed health problems. Then she started washing the priest's cassocks and that kept the family afloat for a few years.

She washed our clothes by hand and that took a toll on her hands and back. But she never failed her task of washing and ironing our clothes!

I can still picture the charcoal iron used in the old days. We used to help her iron the easier pieces of clothing. As there were no daughters, I used to help her in the kitchen and that cooking experience helped when I studied abroad for four years.

To borrow the opening verse of "On Children" by the famous poet Kahlil Gibran:

"Your children are not your children.

They are the sons and daughters of Life's longing for itself.

They come through you but not from you,

And though they are with you, yet they belong not to you".

Set your children free and you too will enjoy the freedom that you deserve. Your children know that you are always there as a source of comfort and safety when a need arises.

Marriage is the most important issue under family matters and there is much to recommend for it. I have been married to a wonderful woman for 37 years now and we have learned to accept each other's foibles.

No spouse is ever perfect for we are all human beings but we have learned how to fight, forgive and carry on in the marriage. My wife sacrificed her career development for more than 12 years to marry me and raise a family. She eventually finished the Association of Chartered Certified Accountants exams when our third daughter was about 4 years old.

That was a major achievement that really helped the family financially.

My father was the person who introduced me to my wife. I would not have met my wife if my father had not obtained her phone number from her father. We both come from Ipoh and were working in Kuala Lumpur.

He had met her father in town and during the conversation, her father gave the phone number so that I could contact her.

The phone number was to enable me to offer her a ride back to Ipoh during my trips home as I used to drive back to Ipoh every few months. I contacted her but she never went back to Ipoh with me until we were going steady.

Of course the fashion now seems to be that there is no need to marry in order to raise a family and many celebrities do just that. You need to evaluate your own circumstances to check if you can follow ALL the celebrities' qualifications before you follow their lifestyle.

Some of them are multi-millionaires with product endorsements that earn them millions each year. So how will you have a baby and take proper care of it when you have to go back to work? Moreover, your boy-friend may ditch you two months after you got pregnant.

Can your parents support you and help take care of the baby? Will they be willing to help and support you after such an episode?

More importantly, what will your social life be like in the future?

For many single mothers, life must surely be quite miserable and lonely as you have few opportunities to socialise and many men will find it difficult to start a long-term relationship with a woman with a child.

We may live in the Facebook era but many men still prefer to marry virgins. So unless you have a very attractive personality, I would encourage girls to say "NO" until you get married.

With a little thinking and willpower, you can always resist the demands for sex before marriage from your partner.

I am sure many are familiar with the reasons a boyfriend uses in order that a girl will give in to him.

"If you love me, you will show it".

"Why don't you prove your love for me?"

"Everyone else is doing it".

"Don't worry, I can take precautions".

"Don't be so old fashioned!"

Please write to the author with other reasons you have heard for people to ask for sex.

Nowadays women are more liberated and may even make the first move so men may need to prepare a defence if they are not ready for sexual relations.

You may be in a relationship but once you have had sex, it is very difficult to keep that strong bond of friendship and most likely you will lose a good friend.

If you have no emotional attachment, it is possible to have a sexual relationship without strings and some people do just that. But I have no information on how long the relationships last. Based on just a convenient sex liaison, I think the relationship could last as long as when the next attractive sex partner comes along.

The concept of a recent movie "No Strings Attached" is hard to practise as people need to connect emotionally for such an intimate relationship. It is also vital to take precautions during sex to avoid getting infected with AIDS and other sexually transmitted diseases.

While casual relationships like one-night stands do more harm than good to your psyche, do not be afraid to fall in love. I believe in the old saying that "it is better to have loved and lost than not to have loved at all."

One other issue about parents is that if you are already an adult, you really cannot blame your parents for whatever problems you have. You need to find out for yourself what you need to do to become an adult who is responsible for his or her actions.

Blaming one's parents has a definite expiry date and I suggest that could range from 18 to 25 years of age.

Taken from Lord Tennyson:

"I hold it true, whate'er befall;

I feel it, when I sorrow most;

'Tis better to have loved and lost

Than never to have loved at all".

Getting a heart broken is painful but it is just part of the human condition and not experiencing it somehow lessens your being as a person.

You can watch a YouTube video "Better to Have Loved" performed by Idina Menzel here. (http://www.youtube.com/watch?v=C9vtjotf7cs)

For older readers, this Nat King Cole's version "Is It Better To Have Loved And Lost?" may be more appropriate. (http://www.youtube.com/watch?v=T4X0nzEaR1U)

Here is a checklist for family matters:

1. Love your parents. Whatever your difficulties, your parents brought you up and did all they could for you.
2. Treat your children fairly. They are God's gift to you and you will be answerable for how they turn out.
3. Ensure that family problems are given a higher priority than other matters.
4. Welcome your children's friends into your house as this is the best method to get to know them.
5. Ensure that the TV and computers and the domestic help do not be become the replacement for the proper nurturing of your children. Be aware of what programs they watch and which web-sites they visit.
6. Children mature at different ages so treat each uniquely. One size fits all does not work with children.
7. Children need some "tough love" so you must be prepared to discipline them in order for them to learn some values.
8. Do not fight in front of the children. The damage to family togetherness could be irreparable.
9. Try to eat family meals together as much as possible. Do not get into the practice of eating at different times unless absolutely necessary. The family meal could be the only time when everyone can get together to share quality time. TV and computers have created a major disruption to eating together as a family.
10. Children are achieving more at a younger age these days like winning Olympics medals and playing professional soccer. You need to look after their special needs more carefully as such early success may not prepare them for a normal life when the dream ends.
11. If you must separate or divorce, do not poison your child's mind by saying nasty things about the absent parent. Your child will grow up with an unhappy disposition as the love

that brought him or her into the world turned into hate and he or she may hate both of you.

12. Your children may decide to marry a person of a different race or religion. Accept your differences and hope they will have a happy life together.

13. Try not to get involved in your married children's lives unless they ask for help. Couples need to learn to work through their problems. Often, well-meaning parents get too involved in their married children's live and complicate things more.

Spiritual Affairs

"There are only two ways to live your life. One is as though nothing is a miracle. The other is as though everything is a miracle." Albert Einstein

Spirituality is another wide area and ranges from a belief in God within or without a religion and includes a non-belief in a God.

I would describe it as how you see your being vis-à-vis the world around you.

People can discover God in various ways even if they have no belief at first. A realisation that a God exists can come from watching a beautiful sunset, waves crashing on a deserted beach or even during a major catastrophe like a tsunami.

Sometimes a person needs to be broken in spirit; maybe he has lost his job or been diagnosed with a dreadful disease. When things look really bleak with no one to help him, he may call God for help in despair.

Those who believe in a God know that it is God who does the actual calling whether or not you believe in his existence.

The faith of a cradle believer is often less than the unbeliever who discovers God and is converted. Such is the nature of human beings. Cradle believers or those who were brought up in a certain faith are more likely to take things for granted. Maybe they need a reminder from God to straighten them out.

Whatever it is, you need to discover the spirituality in your life or you could get entrapped in a life of materialism without any higher dimension. Your soul would be empty and some will consider that you are merely existing; on the same plane as animals.

Illustration 5. Do you need to search
for a higher meaning to life?

I suggest the following to explore the Spiritual area:

1. When you make a friend, ask them about their beliefs in a sensitive manner for religion is quite personal and the person may not want to discuss their religious beliefs. Maybe he or she is also searching like you.
2. You can also walk into a church, mosque or temple and tell the official there that you would like to attend their prayer meeting. Most will welcome you with open arms. For most churches, you can just walk in and sit quietly during the day or you can observe quietly any ceremonies that are going on. Just observe some basic rules like keeping quiet and switching off the mobile phone.
3. This is a simple way to know if you need a religion. In your quiet moments, are you really at peace with yourself and the world around you? Or are you missing something but you cannot define it? For example, if one is hungry you need food to satisfy that need. If you cannot identify what is troubling you, then it could be that your soul is searching for God.
4. Even though you bring up your children in a particular religion, do not expect them to continue in that faith. If they decide to leave, all you can do is pray that they live with the right values and contribute to society. One day they may re-discover the faith that they were brought up in.
5. If you belong to a church, get involved in some church activities. As the saying from the Bible goes: "The harvest is great but the labourers are few". There are many church groups that can make use of your talents.
6. If you do not have quiet moments where you consider the meaning of life, maybe you need to set aside some time to reflect and discover your purpose in life.
7. Whatever your religious beliefs, we all have something powerful called a conscience and that helps everyone live

a life that normally enables one to follow the right path. Everyone has a conscience that acts as a guiding voice but sometimes people ignore their conscience for we all have a free will.

Career Matters

"No man can succeed in a line of endeavour which he does not like". Napoleon Hill

This involves the activities that you will do in order to earn money so that you can enjoy the lifestyle you want. It may be a business or a job. If you are the heir to a large fortune, this may not apply but you will still have to learn to manage your wealth.

Most jobs are mundane with many repetitive tasks and demanding bosses who do not really appreciate the problems you face. But that's why they paid you – so that they do not have to handle those problems themselves.

Illustration 6. Encourage your child to read

My experience:

I did not inherit any wealth so I have no idea of what the issues of inheritance are. Maybe you will have relatives or close friends hoping that you will spare some of your largesse or fortune.

Unlike many of my friends, no one paid anything for my first car or house; it was all based on savings and loans.

I have worked many years in different companies of different industries like food, pharmaceuticals, rubber and plantations.

Looking back, I know I could have made better, more satisfying choices.

The most significant work I did was as a development engineer and I helped the company produce an automatic rubber processing machine that was patented. The company that produces the rubber product called Linatex had sent Malaysians to the UK as part of the program to replace expatriates. I stayed there for more than 6 years but the replacement program for expatriates progressed at a snail's pace.

It was quite difficult to leave the first company as both the Managing Director and General Manager were like father figures and I joined the company straight after leaving Sixth Form at St. Michael's Institution in Ipoh.

But I felt it was necessary to leave to develop my career further and so I resigned.

I would make the following suggestions for anyone's sound career progression:

1. It is not worth changing jobs for just a few extra dollars. Career development and future prospects are more important.

2. Try to stay in a new job for at least two years so that you can learn something in depth and will not be perceived to be a job hopper. You cannot dispel the notion that you are a job hopper by the recruiting manager when you submit your application. You may not even get a chance at an interview to explain your reasons for the frequent job changes.

3. Try and find a mentor. It must be a person you can trust who will be able to guide you in your career or business development. Even top badminton players need coaches, so having a mentor should help your career.

4. Never fight with your superior. It is a battle that you cannot win. If you resign with a blow-up and bad feelings, realise that any referrals will make you look bad. Who do you think is going to write the details of your performance?

5. Stay current in your profession and attend courses regularly. Ask your company if it sponsors training programs. Pay for your own career development if the company does not sponsor such courses.

6. Work hard and look for opportunities to show your skills and be noticed by your boss and senior management. Volunteer for cross-divisional projects that give you the opportunity to network and work with colleagues from different parts of the organisation.

7. Appraisals are a good time to evaluate your prospects with the company and also the company's future. Never assume that everything remains the same. Business moves fast and you do not want to be in a company that has no vision.

Financial Matters

"It's good to have money and the things that money can buy, but it's good, too, to check up once in a while and make sure that you haven't lost the things that money can't buy." George Lorimer

Whether you are interested in money or not, you need to be able to manage your finances so that it will not interfere in other areas that you find more interesting.

One simple rule about not becoming bankrupt is that your spending must never exceed your earnings on a regular basis. For example, a person earning $2000 per month and manages to save $200 each month will have more money in the bank after one year than a person who earns $5000 and saves only $50 per month.

Parents are the first teachers of all matters, including how to manage money. Children can be taught the value of money from an early age. When you give a child pocket money, you can encourage him to put some away for spending later.

Open a savings account at the bank so that he understands how money flows in the economy. If your child requests for extra money, you can ask him to do simple chores like helping you to wash the car or clean the toilets even if you have a paid helper or cleaner.

Illustration 7. Teach your children the value of money and they will attain the mastery of money.

My story:

My father worked as a Chief Clerk in a government department but his salary was hardly enough to provide for his large family of five children.

My mother did not work but instead took care of the house, cooking and cleaning on an inadequate budget. It was a heart-breaking existence, with hardly any time and money for recreation.

When I was on scholarship in the UK from 1967 to 1971, I had to be very careful with money as there was only the scholarship money to pay for living expenses with no support from home. We used to get about RM500 each month and I used to send home about RM40 each month to support the family as I still had two younger brothers in school. It was really no big deal as I managed to save and buy my first car over there for about GBP85. I was even able to join two week-long vacations in the UK organised by the British Council and the Edinburgh Festival was one of the highlights.

During one December holidays, I even worked as a temporary postman delivering Christmas cards. There is no truth in the adventures of a postman except there are some very strong letter slots that will slam on your fingers!

Just before my final year, I took a 16-day trip to Europe with Cosmos, the leading tour company at the time.

If you asked me to describe my thrift habits, I would say that I can be very stingy. My mother used to refer to me as the "Scottish Jew" but I did not take offence. To me, being careful with money is very important as I still have scars since childhood for lack of money.

Wasting food is considered a crime and we still eat overnight food. I can still faintly remember the distant times when I curled up under the bed to sleep as I was so hungry. Dinner had been delayed as my father had not returned home with some money to buy the food.

Getting the first pay-check is always exciting and usually your family and friend may ask for a treat. It is OK to indulge them just once. After that you need to take charge of your money or money problems will take charge of your life. Control money or the debts will consume you and make life unbearable.

My suggestions for handling financial matters are:

1. Live within your means and you will never get into financial difficulties.
2. Never be a borrower or lender. You can lose friends that way. Of course you need a bank loan to buy a house. Just ensure your income is adequate to meet future instalments.
3. Save some of your salary or business proceeds so that you can survive for three to six months in case your earnings fall; from loss of job or business slow-down. There is no guarantee that your company does not downsize or that the economy will not tank. Be prepared with this emergency fund.
4. Once you have secured the emergency fund, you should consider saving for the deposit on a house. Owning a house can be an important step into creating wealth for the future. When buying properties, the most important factor is "location, location, location"; especially when you are not going to live there yourself.
5. Do the maths properly to check if buying or renting a house makes good financial sense.
6. Borrowing money from loan sharks is a "no-no". You will be badly hit and possibly killed if you do not pay up.
7. If you cannot control your spending, do not own a credit card as it is always easy to buy more things on credit. Always

pay the monthly balance in full so you do not incur penalty charges and pay interest charges of 2% per month. Credit card companies value their customers so ask them to waive the credit card annual fees and most card companies oblige but you need to ask.

8. You can save a lot if you stock up on loss leaders from supermarkets if you use the products on offer regularly; these are items that you already have used and enjoy the quality. Calculate the cost per unit weight of each packaging size. Usually the bigger the package, the lower the unit price but please check the maths as some places have irrational pricing!

9. Learn to buy stocks and shares; based on your risk appetite. I have the following criteria before I buy a stock. Good management, 5-years track record of consistent profits, low debts, and low price to book ratio. Reading current affairs can also give some insight into what companies will do well. The best performing stock I bought was a glove company during the SARs epidemic in 2002. When the company declared a bonus issue, I took out my original capital and bought a plantation stock that has since doubled in value. The residual stock in the glove company still exceeds the original capital. I have held stocks in a company for more than 30 years!

10. Do your own research for investment decisions. I never ask my broker for stock advice. I will always tell friends who offered hot tips. "Even if the Finance Minister gives me stock tips, the information is not really useful for me unless I know what his position in the market was". Before you follow any such tip, you need to ask yourself: "How many thousands have heard this rumour before me?"

11. Don't lose any money gambling – the deck is always stacked against you. If you must put some money into gambling,

buy a gambling stock like Genting in Malaysia. That way you will at least get a share of their winnings.

12. There is no free lunch in life and many "get rich quick" schemes abound. Any company that promises wealth based mainly on continuous recruitment is a Ponzi scheme. The trouble is that even some of your friends get taken in by such schemes. I am not sure what the ratio of products consumed/members recruited should be to get any company classified as a Ponzi scheme but I suggest a 70/30 ratio is a safe one to ensure that your main activity is actually distributing products. Beware of any company that boasts "No more fees if you recruit 4 or more active members". Of course the early members may make lots of money but ultimately the bubble will burst. Do you want to be left holding the empty bag? Even worse, you could have got your friends to part with their hard-earned savings!

13. Buy quality clothes and shoes for they last longer. Go for quality rather than the brand. Clothes with a classic look can be used longer as they do not go out of fashion.

14. Make a will as soon as you start working for you will already own assets. A will can ease the burden of the ones you leave behind as there will be fewer disputes over how your estate will be disposed.

Social Matters

"The hardest job kids face today is learning good manners without seeing any." Fred Astaire

Unless you live in a cave, you will need to mingle in society and learn how to interact with your co-workers and service providers like the gardener, the repairman, the waitress and the car mechanic; amongst others. You need to learn the language and the norms followed by society or people will get the impression that you did come from a cave.

Nowadays it is much harder to make friends by getting to know strangers as everyone is too busy with their smart phones and texting or face-booking that they may miss the opportunity to make a friend. By not paying full attention to what is going on around them, they endanger themselves-a thief may be stalking them or you might even fall into an open manhole like the girl in China. Maybe we should encourage "Make a Friend Week" during which people will not use their hand-phones while using public transport and walking in parks and public places.

I worry that some folks nowadays are so obsessed with their gadgets that they are not aware that the birds are singing and the flowers are in full bloom. We all need some time to smell the flowers or watch a beautiful sunset.

Illustration 8. The family meal is so important for bonding - pay attention to your loved ones

My experience:

I had a wonderful experience in the United Kingdom more than 40 years ago. During the 6-months industrial training, I used to walk to the factory from my bed-sitter, a distance of about three kilometres. After a few weeks, I noticed a beautiful girl that walked in the opposite direction.

She had long blonde hair and a nice figure.

I admired her each day as she dressed quite smartly with high boots and she used to carry a small basket (sandwiches for lunch?). After a few days she looked back at me and we exchanged smiles every day after that.

That would be the highlight for the day and I made sure I left my house at the correct time so that I would pass her in the 500meters where our paths crossed; only for maybe 10 seconds.

I was such a novice at approaching girls that only after several days of exchanging smiles did I summon the courage to say "Hi!"

What spurred me on was the knowledge that I would be leaving for my Europe holiday in two days and after that I would be shifting back to Portsmouth to continue the course. She responded to my greeting and we soon became friends.

Isn't the saying true? "A stranger is a friend you have not met".

The moral of the story is you must take some action if you want results. Be open to making friends by being the first to smile or start a conversation.

Politeness is appreciated by everyone and these are some ways to practise your social skills:

1. Always let people exit before you enter a lift or a train carriage, as trying to enter when people are exiting is bad manners. Manners make the man or woman! When someone opens a door for you, give a friendly "Thank you".

2. Park your car in a proper place. Double-parking creates traffic congestion and upsets everyone. Walk a little if you have to.

3. Never beat the red light. I have seen too many accidents caused by drivers accelerating after the light turned red.

4. Dress smartly and appropriately for any function. Practise good hygiene and ask a close friend or family member if you have body odour or bad breath. These can be treated-if not your smell could put people off.

5. Join a club or activity where you can meet others in a social setting. This could be a hiking club, a community choir or a Toastmasters Club. I know three couples who met in Toastmasters and are now happily married. At a Toastmasters meeting, you develop and practise public speaking and leadership skills. These skills are vital for anyone who wants to improve his prospects for promotion. Kill two birds with one stone in a Toastmasters club. Usually the people who join a TM club are positive and encouraging-become a member for at least two years and your life will be transformed!

6. If you are married, you need to set some priorities so as not to upset the family equilibrium. If your spouse joins your social activities, it is so much the better. But it is also possible for each one to enjoy social activities separately. You need to develop trust in each other or your marriage will suffer.

7. If you are single and interested in a member of the opposite sex, there is nothing wrong with going up to a person, giving

a nice smile and saying "Hello". If the person responds positively by giving you a friendly smile back, you can introduce yourself and make some polite conversation. With some practice and a few gaffes, you will develop the skill of knowing how prepared the other person is for a relationship. Have you ever wondered why you can see some couples that appear very mismatched? Like a very beautiful girl going with a rather wimpy guy? It's because too many guys were intimidated by her beauty and everyone assumed that she must have a boy-friend! And the poor girl might have been just waiting for someone nice to ask her.

Health Matters

"The first wealth is health." **Ralph Waldo Emerson**

There is a perennial debate over which is more important – health or wealth. One side argues that wealth is more important than health as money can buy the best medicine and pay for the best doctors. I prefer the other argument that health is more important. With good health you can concentrate on the important things that can bring you great wealth.

Illustration 9. You are responsible for taking care of yourself!

My experience:

I played many sports when young; especially badminton which I did not give up until the age of forty-five years when I suffered a slipped disc while carrying furniture. In school, I played soccer, hockey and even rugby though soccer was the favourite.

I never did get the hang of the hockey stick with the offside rules and rugby was a one-off game. I had difficulty getting down in the centre of the scrum. The problem was in Sixth Form, if you are active in sports, the same chaps get recruited for a variety of team sports.

Walking was another sport I was good at. I remember winning the class prize for a 12km school walk in Ipoh. While in college, I walked the 40km from Portsmouth to Southampton as part of the Student's Week and raised GBP25 for charity. It took a record time of 9 hours!

I have taken part in the Malay Mail Big Walk in Kuala Lumpur twice and managed to finish within the qualifying time for the age group.

Nowadays my exercise is swimming at least twice a week to keep fit.

As one gets older, various health issues arise. Get advice from your doctor but try and get alternative views if possible. Doctors too can make serious mistakes.

This is what happened to my wife.

She had drooping eyelids and consulted a specialist who diagnosed it as myasthenia gravis, a serious neuromuscular disorder that could be fatal; and was given a cocktail of medications until the blood tests came back.

So we did a lot of Googling and decided to consult the Singapore National Eye Centre. The doctor there gave a chuckle and advised my wife that the other doctor had made an error. The reason for the drooping eyes was that my wife spent long hours at the computer and rubbed her eyes too vigorously when they became itchy.

The rubbing damaged the delicate muscles around the eyelids and hence the drooping. Two quick operations solved that medical problem.

Needless to say, we did not go back to the first doctor for further consultations!

If you have health problems, it is important to take the proper medications for some diseases can be fatal.

We moved from Johor Baru city to the suburbs in 2010 but sometimes I still go to the Tebrau Market to visit the familiar stalls.

I last saw the pork seller in June 2012. He was quite a jovial man about 67 years old and had a daughter who had migrated to the UK after marrying an Englishman.

On 26th August 2012, I wanted to buy some pork but when I reached his stall, I found it empty. The next stall holder told me he had passed away. So I asked: "What happened?"

He said that the old man had taken some sex stimulants from China and that had killed him.

Here are some ways to stay healthy:

1. Eat moderately and enjoy a healthy diet with all the major food groups. It is better to eat less but more frequently; rather than large meals. Limit your intake of sugar - excess soft drinks with high sugar content is a modern health problem that is causing serious obesity problems on a global scale.

2. Chew your food properly and take some food supplements for a balanced diet.

3. Exercise regularly and it will become a healthy habit. Swimming and brisk walks can be done solo or you can play games like badminton, tennis and even soccer.

4. Get enough sleep or your next day could be unproductive and even dangerous if you doze off at the wheel of your car. I have experienced "sleep driving". You drive some distance and when you arrive at a certain point, you realise that you were not fully conscious of the journey. If you feel sleepy while driving, park your vehicle and take a short nap. Even a 10-minute break can work wonders!

5. Do not drink and drive. The ride may be thrilling but the chances of an accident are much higher as your judgement is impaired with alcohol.

6. Learn to cook simple meals as this will be healthier than the food you buy.

7. Get into the habit of emptying your bowels at least once a day so that your body is cleared of waste products each day.

8. Get a medical check-up at least once a year and see your dentist at least once in six months.

9. Death is a certainty but we do not know the time, the place or how life will end. So accept its inevitability, take good care of your health and live a life of purpose.

Educational Matters

"An education isn't how much you have committed to memory, or even how much you know. It's being able to differentiate between what you know and what you don't." **Anatole France**

It is important that you attain the highest education standard possible before you apply for a job anywhere. Once you work for a few years, it get harder to return to study but not impossible.

Illustration 10. Encourage your child to develop life-long learning habits

My experience:

My wife returned to complete the Association of Chartered Certified Accountants exams when our third daughter was about 3 years old. It was tough but she was motivated by her need to break through the "glass ceiling" as she was a non-graduate.

Family help is important and my mother was able to stay with us for two years while my wife spent most of her time studying. It did not help that we lived in Petaling Jaya while the college was in Ampang, about 40km away and there were no highways between those towns then.

It is good to pursue a course of study that you are interested in. If you work in a job that you truly enjoy, then it is not work anymore. The bonus is that you get paid for doing something you really enjoy.

I was lucky that I studied in the same school for 13 years; at St. Michael's Institution from Primary 1 right through to Sixth Form.

School was not a major problem for me. The main problem was that my family was so poor that sometimes we never knew where the next meal was coming from.

Luckily, a family friend helped us to get exemption from paying school fees or most of us would have dropped out from school. My godparents, who did not have children, took us in and shared their home with us when we had to move out of government quarters after my father retired. I suspect my godmother always cooked extra as she knew that we did not have enough to eat. We shared a house for about 10 years during my teenage years.

The school years were tough but I managed to survive and did reasonably well in my studies. I did not go to kindergarten nor did I get any tuition during the entire school years. I would describe my study method as being a plodder. I was envious of those who got the same results by cramming for exams just three weeks before.

Still my results were satisfactory but not consistent. I topped the class in Primary 1 and got a double promotion to Primary 3. I can still remember when I topped the class in Primary 3, the Head-Master chided the class as it contained the brightest pupils. I also did well in Form 1 and 3; topping the whole school a few times during the monthly tests. Many students joined the class from other schools from Form 4 and then onwards the competition became more intense. These brighter students had been promoted to my school that was considered a premier school in Ipoh.

I managed to be one of only four students in my school admitted to Sixth Form after the Entrance Test; the others had to join after the MCE results. The Entrance Exams results were published in the press and I was placed at the 15th position in Perak state. I believe some of the Form 5 teachers were quite surprised at the results.

In Form 6, girls joined the school and for me it was nice but since my parents had five sons, I was rather poor at "tackling the girls" even though a few became good friends. After Sixth Form, I managed to get a four-year scholarship after a very competitive selection process that included a 28-day course at the Outward Bound School in Lumut.

In those days, teenagers were given very little sex information as parents considered sex a taboo subject or they assumed you would learn about it when the time came?

The following personal stories show the importance of being correctly educated about sex. Of course kids nowadays can learn so much sex online and often they will know more than some adults who are reluctant to discuss this important subject.

Parents should be well aware of their kids' sexuality and be prepared to share their knowledge when the time is appropriate.

I remember I was about 13 years old when I asked my godmother: "What does the word "r-a-p-e" mean?" I had read an article in the newspapers. She told me it was nothing to worry about.

Before I left on my scholarship to the UK, I had this advice from an aunt: "Don't get involved with the English girls".

This incident may shock you but it is worth telling.

I was studying in Portsmouth Polytechnic and the college does not have a separate campus. After lunch in the student's cafeteria, I used to walk in the city centre, window-shopping as the displays were quite attractive.

On one of these walks, a middle-aged Englishman came over and said "Hello" with a friendly smile. I said "Hello" and he invited me for a drink. Thinking he was just a local trying to be friendly with a foreign student, I accepted as I thought a refusal might appear rude.

We went into a small basement pub and he ordered two pints of beer. As we were drinking, he tells me: "I like you and you have a nice face."

No one had ever given me such a compliment before and suddenly, I had a queer feeling.

When the drinks were almost finished, he asked me: "Would you like to go somewhere else?" My mind was now racing as to what should be my course of action. I told him I needed to go to the toilet first and got up and took my umbrella with me. While he was settling the bill, I darted up the stairs and made a quick exit. I did not look back but I think the man was not really harmful.

My four children had different career paths that were influenced by study choices and also financial constraints.

We were fortunate that the first two daughters were admitted into Singapore universities and completed their degrees. Both obtained tuition grants from the government and so the fees were reduced.

My third daughter had always wanted to study medicine and my dear wife managed to save enough to send her to medical school. She did a transfer program from International Medical University to Dalhousie University in Canada. She has happily settled down in Canada. I do not recommend forcing a child to study medicine for the course is so arduous and expensive.

My youngest, the son, also was unsure of a career choice until he had to return from Singapore to do "A" levels in Malaysia. Apart from Mathematics, he chose Law, Accounting and Economics which were new subjects for him. He had not been an avid reader so we were pleasantly surprised he wanted to do a Law degree! He was so interested in the subject that he would take his law books to read in bed.

One other activity that all my children did was to take piano lessons. Unfortunately all three girls dropped at various stages; partly from lack of interest or mostly to concentrate on scoring higher marks in exams.

As my son had a seven-year gap from the youngest girl, we did not ask him to learn the piano as we felt that he would also give up like the other siblings. Luckily we did not sell the piano as when he was in Primary 6, he asked for music lessons! To his credit, he took lessons and passed Grade 8 piano and that was the highest grade among the children.

It is nice at family gatherings especially Christmas to hear the children sing carols. My son and third daughter even sang a duet at my second daughter's wedding.

I suggest you to do the following to help maintain balance in education:

1. Pay attention in class and don't waste time in idle talk. Try and do homework in class so you are free to do other things when you get home.
2. There is no point questioning the teacher if you just happen to know more than him or her. Having to handle a class with more than thirty students is no mean feat. But you can ask to speak to the teacher in private if you have questions.
3. Do your own work and do not copy anyone. That person may be having all the wrong answers. It is better to get fewer marks in an exam than to copy so you know your true standard. Without knowing how weak you are, you cannot take the proper steps to remedy the problem.
4. Try to be friendly to everyone but choose a handful that you can be close friends with. If you attend a mixed school, do not be awkward with the opposite sex but treat them with respect and you will develop a balanced personality.
5. Be obliging and helpful to the teachers but don't try to be a teacher's pet. Be courteous and don't taunt the teacher. I once witnessed an angry teacher take down a student who was rude and hold him with a judo lock. I can still hear the loud noise when the teacher slammed the student down on the wooden floor! In those days, no one questioned the teachers' abuse.

6. Research the courses and universities you wish to attend and what results you will need to be accepted. Tell your parents early on and discuss with them the options to achieve your goal. Be aware that competition to get into top universities is intense and the cost is high. Spend time during the long holidays on this research so that by Secondary Five, you have already selected the course/s you want to do.

7. Develop a habit of reading good books of any genre and you will go far. Don't play so many computer games and I suggest you create a list of good books to read. Try to complete at least one book per month.

8. Get involved in your child's Parent-Teachers Association for schools need help from parents to ensure children get the best education possible.

9. Studying music helps your child to study better so try and encourage your child to take up a music course as it helps to exercise both left and right brain. There is music even specially composed to help children study well-it is quite different from pop music! Music should be treated as a recreation and not a chore or the child will not benefit much.

10. Before you send your children for studies overseas, you need to sit down and have a good chat with your son or daughter to see if there are any areas in sex education that need to be elaborated on.

Recreational Matters

"If bread is the first necessity of life, recreation is a close second". **Edward Bellamy**

I would describe recreation as activities that you participate in purely for the sake of your personal enjoyment. So tagging along with your wife on her shopping spree may or may not be considered recreation!

Recreation is something we should all learn to enjoy as it is something relatively new. In the old days, there was hardly any recreation enjoyed by ordinary folks. The wealthy have always enjoyed their recreation; from hunting foxes to having grand parties.

Nowadays with more machines to do the heavy work and with many tasks being automated, we do not have to work such long hours. Recreational time is important as you can enrich your life by taking part in activities that give enjoyment and satisfaction. Not everyone works in a job that is truly 100% satisfying but you stay at that job mainly to earn money and spend the surplus on your recreational activities!

Watching TV as the only recreation is very limiting and you should not spend all your free time in front of the idiot box. It is bad for health and the only people who gain are the cable television networks.

You need to spend quality time with your family or your bond of kinship may not be strong enough to sustain you in times of crisis.

Illustration 11. It's important to spend quality time with your family

My experience:

I discovered a hobby that has enabled me to raise funds for charity. After the 2004 tsunami in Indonesia, I decided that giving money would be the most practical way to help them. Unless you are a doctor or health worker who is properly trained, going to a disaster area is not recommended as you would be more a hindrance than a help.

I decided to bake pineapple tarts to sell to friends and neighbours. I priced them at a slight premium and donated half of the proceeds to charity. Since then I have used this method to raise funds whenever there is a major disaster like floods and earthquakes. So even if you are a one-man show, you can still contribute.

For the recreational area, I suggest the following:

1. If you enjoy an activity like gardening or cooking, read up on the subject so that you become better at it. The better your results, the more you will enjoy your recreation.
2. Some people even turn their recreation into a business that can really take off so that they even quit their day jobs. You need a lot of exploring and research of your own needs before you embark on this change. Sometimes a lot of the enjoyment will disappear when the stress of running a business takes over.
3. Make sure you do not spend so much time and money on your recreation that it becomes an obsession that impacts the other areas of your life. For example, if you enjoy horse racing, you might become a race-course addict and spend all your money gambling.
4. Be adventurous and have no regrets. It is better to try something once than forever live in regret at your timidity.

5. Explore the different activities you can join for your recreation and enjoy! Life is meant to be worth living. Try out new hobbies and you may discover a love of music, singing or painting.

6. Travel always broadens your mind and gives you a better perspective of what is happening in the world. Explore the ancient civilisations in places like Machu Picchu, the Pyramids, Borobudur and Angkor Wat. Spend a week or a month volunteering in a poor country.

7. Learning a new language can be very enriching and can open up new areas to enrich your life.

8. If you are lazy or not creative enough to do your own research into recreation ask your friends what they do for a hobby so that you can also try it. You might be surprised at the rich variety of hobbies that people do! Of course they will not disclose if they are illegal bookies; so be a little discreet about it.

Differences between Life and Sudoku

Now that we have explored all the areas in the Sudoku matrix, please bear in mind that these eight areas are based on my experience and values and you should create your own important areas that affect your life.

When you solve a Sudoku puzzle, sometimes you find that it is easy to fill in one particular number like all the "1"s in the relevant squares. In life too, you may find that you will find a particular trait you have that is useful in many areas. Make use of it as much as possible but generally you find that alone will not solve the puzzle.

With a Sudoku puzzle, you can also check out a particular answer when you have to make a 50:50 decision. Sometimes even with one answer checked correctly you find that you cannot solve the puzzle.

In life you will face challenges that you need help with. There is nothing wrong with asking for help but it is important that you get clarity on the problem first or you might get an answer or solution for the wrong problem. However, it is still better to try out a solution than to keep avoiding the problem by not doing anything.

With a Sudoku puzzle you sometimes have a breakthrough number and suddenly you find that you can fill all the correct spaces with that number and that may result in a quicker solution. In life, you may similarly get a breakthrough and discover that a certain talent may be easily applied in all the areas and that may create a faster life-work balance. That talent may be caring for others or perhaps good time management.

I have written about life's matrix based on my own script. Each one of us is unique and no two life scripts are identical. That is what makes each person's life so interesting but unfortunately not many people are able or willing to share that experience for we can all learn so much from each other.

It is your life and you could even create a larger matrix. Your important areas could be children, politics, or even sports. You decide on what you want in the matrix.

This is your life and you should make plans that meet your requirements. Some parts of your script cannot be changed as your current situation is the culmination of all the decisions you made in the past combined with the set of conditions that you were born with.

Fortunately for humans, your past does not dictate your future. You have a choice and when you make a decision to act, you will gain better control of your life. When you tell your friends about impending changes in your life, be prepared for discouraging remarks; even from your family and close friends.

At times your friends may be afraid to lose your friendship if you succeed.

This quote is most apt:

Never allow a person to tell you "NO" who doesn't have the power to say" yes".

Eleanor Roosevelt

Life changes like a Sudoku puzzle. When you feel your life is good and in equilibrium, change happens and that is inevitable! So you need to solve another matrix in order to get balance in your life again.

The only difference is this: For Sudoku fans, you can choose the difficulty of the puzzle you want to solve but in life, the puzzle you are dealt with is random and could have a positive or negative effect on your equilibrium. For example, if you are a surprise winner of $50 million, I am sure your life would need re-balancing. Other major life-changing events would be getting married, having a first child, losing your job or migrating.

When you cannot solve a Sudoku puzzle and it is messed up with mistakes, it takes longer to solve. A puzzle can be put aside for a few hours or days and it is OK.

You can check in the answers section if you want to choose between 2 squares so the mess does not get too great but really if you use a pencil, you can always indicate when you made a 50/50 decision.

When you face difficulties you can ask friends and family for help. Spending some quiet time to reflect on your problems could also help bring clarity and sometimes a solution may present itself. But unlike a Sudoku puzzle, life goes on and if you ignore your problems, they will not disappear.

In a Sudoku puzzle there is only one correct answer whereas in life there are different possible answers as you can choose the solution that fits your needs. Life is full of compromises and making decisions based on the facts you have.

A Sudoku puzzle represents a particular phase in your life and can represent a day, a week, and months or even years when your life is out of balance. After you solve one puzzle, you are better prepared to solve the next puzzle.

With Sudoku, you can select the difficulty of each puzzle as the problems are usually graded from easy to challenging. Life is not like that – an easy puzzle can be followed by one that is extremely difficult.

When you can solve the positions of a particular number in Sudoku, you should do so without worrying about the other eight numbers. Don't spend too much time trying to find all the positions for a particular number if it takes too long but go on to the next number. This improves your time management skills.

When you find the position for any number, you must be prepared to leave that square and shift to the new square. In life you need to leave your comfort zone and try out new areas to get a better life-work balance.

When you solve a puzzle, it is surprising that often the puzzle is not solved in the sequence you expected; for example the square with the most given numbers may not be completed before other areas are solved. In life too, it is quite possible that the area where you expected the least problems could be the one that is hardest to resolve.

Sudoku trains you to focus and also multi-task in the background for you must realise all the other numbers are required to solve the puzzle.

Sometimes, you wonder just how a particular number fits in the solution for Sudoku. In life, it is similar when you wonder about the purpose of a new skill you have learned.

Whatever advice I have given here is based only on my life experience. Please feel free to challenge them and what is more important, to develop your own beliefs. Writing your beliefs in a book will give you more conviction about your values and really strengthen your CORE.

Having a strong CORE is important as it can sustain you with the many challenges that life brings.

I still struggle to balance my life and it is definitely more difficult than solving Sudoku puzzles. Some of those suggestions are also my own self-talk to help me improve and may not apply to everyone.

The few numbers that are given in the Sudoku puzzle represent the CORE values that affect you. These values can be in any area of the puzzle and you need them to solve each puzzle.

Changes in your life are inevitable and if you understand the concept of "Life is Like a Sudoku Puzzle", you will be prepared for any challenge that arises.

Being an expert Sudoku solver is no guarantee that you will be an expert solver of life's problems but it does help you to improve your thinking skills.

Encourage your children to solve Sudoku puzzles, their concentration span will definitely improve.

Maybe they will become curious and want to try when they see you enjoying the puzzles but do start them with the simpler puzzles.

Life is exciting....Embrace it!

Each one of us is a unique human being, endowed with unique qualities and capable of changing the world in different ways. No one can take the special role you are meant to contribute.

If all the Bill Gates or Steve Jobs of the world did not write their own script for life and persisted with passion, the world will be a different place today.

This book can help to re-balance your life but you have to work out your own script. No one else can do it for you and reading another 20 motivational books will not work unless you actually get down to a serious script that works for you.

You are the master of your destiny but you need to plan your journey. It is important to make a start somewhere and you should not wait until all the conditions are perfect.

This quote is attributable to Mark Twain:

> *"Twenty years from now you will be more disappointed by the things that you didn't do than by the ones you did do. So throw off the bowlines. Sail away from the safe harbour. Catch the trade winds in your sails. Explore. Dream. Discover."*

Readers Feedback

"My old friend Harold, through personal anecdotes, experience and extensive reading, shares some gems of wisdom for young and old in this insightful little book."

> Gerad Carrier- Florida, USA. School Administrator, International Educator.

"A simple-to-read book that offers much sensible advice. I applaud and appreciate Harold's insight and sharing of his numerous life experiences. This book is a compelling read, but more importantly, it's a valuable tool for us to reflect and refocus our CORE values."

> Lee-Jean Fung, founder of My Pharmacy, Malaysia

"Simple and Comprehensible. Although this book targets a younger generation who are starting life , it is a good read for everyone of all ages. The book is plainly written with gems of advice on how to lead a successful life – spiritually, physically and holistically.

Harold espouses to the readers the need to strike a successful balance between work, career development and the needs of their families.

His analogy of life's activities, problems and strategies with Sudoku is also interesting, and provides a different way of assisting us through life's problems.

Harold has very humbly and honestly shared his own experiences with his readers in an effort to portray his concepts and approach to life as ongoing as well as a learning process".

> Prof. Dr. Farida Habib Shah – Malaysia.
> Fellow,The World Academy of Science (TWAS).
> Founder of The Natural Story- A herbal wellness manufacturing company

"In Life is Like a Book of Sudoku, Harold Angus mapped his life experiences to the boxes and the numbers of Sudoku and told it in the most interesting but honest way. The game of Sudoku begins with a given set of numbers, so does life with its preconditions, those one to accept, cherish and make use of towards betterment. Sudoku is about solving dilemmas, having options and choosing the most appropriate where one may or may not succeed but to Harold, this is also what life is. Sudoku is a life's miniature as Harold sees it and this makes an entertaining yet motivational read, a must get".

> Airil Yasreen Yassin, PhD -Johor Baru, Malaysia. Researcher, university lecturer, blogger

"There is much wisdom in Life is Like a Book of Sudoku. If you have not done the Sudoku yet you would probably be curious enough to want to do so after reading this easy-to-read guide to life. As you go on in life, many mistakes will be made, but with Life is Like a Book of Sudoku, be assured that lessons can be learnt from Harold's life experiences which you can easily relate to, and make going through life, one with the occasional obstacle, more of a breeze.

Life is Like a Book of Sudoku is a personal encounter warmly shared with the public, entertaining, witty and light-hearted. I recommend reading it.

Noor Azimah Abdul Rahim, Chairman of PAGE (Malaysia)

"An interesting easy read, full of good advice for the young and "not so young".

Once I started, I couldn't put it down.

People everywhere are the same, regardless of origin, facing constant change and challenges as we grow and mature. It's a small beautiful world and we must strive to leave it better than it was before us. Harold's book is certainly a legacy for generations to come. Congratulations!"

Waleska Wray, Ohio, USA. Language Arts teacher, Banking Administration Officer, Financial Specialist.

"It is the story of the author's life journey. His experiences on the path he took tell of the success and failure that he went through to get to where he is now.

The book contains a wealth of information and ideas about living and it may help the reader to understand the value of education, friendship, marriage, spirituality and the other challenges. As a whole it would give the reader valuable knowledge on life.

We never know what our destinies are but we can learn from others' experiences so as to understand what living is all about.

Idrus Abu Bakar-Kuala Lumpur, Malaysia. A Social change activist

"My former classmate Harold's book covers life topics like career, health, financial management and education. It takes time, strategy, effort and perseverance to live and enjoy life.

You don't need to be able to solve Sudoku puzzles to enjoy and learn from Harold's book. After you finish the book you, like me might still suck at the Japanese invention but you would have learned something and had a few laughs."

Patrick Teoh-Kuala Lumpur, Malaysia.
Actor, irregular Writer.

Conclusion

If this book succeeded in giving you a fresh outlook how to re-invent your life and enabled you to refocus on your CORE values, then I would consider it a success.

Yes, life is indeed like a book of Sudoku that must be done by everyone!

Now you can go out and face life's challenges with greater confidence.

I wish to thank the following:

Partridge Singapore for helping to bring this book to fruition.

Gerad Carrier, Jean Angus and my dear wife for improving the script and correcting errors.

Dave Fisher for permission to use the Sudoku puzzle.

The Readers who offered encouraging comments.

Thank you for reading this book. All errors are entirely my fault. Any suggestions or criticisms can be sent to lilabos47@yahoo.com.